WHAT HAPPENED AT THE END OF THE ROAD

a poetry collection

WARŨGŨRŨ MŨCHĨRA

Published in Nairobi, Kenya by
THE OLD MOSS

ISBN: 978-9914-49-356-6

This is a work of fiction. Names, characters, businesses, places, events and incidents are either the products of the author's imagination or used in a fictitious manner. Any resemblance to actual persons, living or dead, or actual events is purely coincidental.

Cover Design
Polka Creatives

Author's Note
This collection includes new work as well as revised content originally published via ictrn.com and the following Instagram accounts:
@warugurumuchira and @sundayschildke

Printed in Nairobi, Kenya by
Brandworld Communications Ltd.

WHAT HAPPENED AT THE END OF THE ROAD

THE OLD MOSS

WHAT HAPPENED AT THE END OF THE ROAD

Warũgũrũ Mũchĩra was born and raised in Nairobi, Kenya. The fourth in a family of five, she is a former Business Correspondent for the Daily Nation, a former contributor to True Love East Africa magazine and was briefly a Business Writer at the Star. Her children's story, Akinyi, was longlisted for the Golden Baobab Prize in 2018.

Warũgũrũ holds a degree in Education from the Catholic University of Eastern Africa and is an alumna of Strathmore University.

What Happened at the End of the Road is her first poetry collection.

For every hurting, hopeful heart
journeying to light and healing

they asked her
how did you come this far
she answered
my every stepping stone was a star

CONTENTS

I. THE END OF THE ROAD

II. INTO THE DARK

III. GLIMMERS

IV. INTO THE LIGHT

“With all its sham, drudgery and broken dreams, it is still a beautiful world.”

Max Ehrmann

“At the end of the road, the way appears.”

Maya Angelou

“Isn't it funny how day by day nothing changes, but when you look back, everything is different.”

C.S. Lewis

I

THE END OF THE ROAD

Cloud Formation

Now they sit in silence
and look at each other
but neither one
sees the other.

Of Monsters & Men

The monster was always there
hiding in plain sight
as obvious as the dark of night

but sweet words and pretty things
blinded her to the ugly that lurked within
gently drew her in

then slowly the truth rose to the surface
as degree by degree the mask slipped out of place
and she came to see that whom she'd loved
was an illusion
a well practiced deception
delivered poker faced

childhood monsters that hid in the dark
running riot in her head
all paled in comparison
to the real life horror she'd come to dread
the ogre that lay next to her in bed.

Dead Wood

How easily you lie
master of guile
son of deceit
with as many faces
as that angel with cloven feet

one lie flows into another
consigning you to the depths of hell
a thousand by a thousand measures
about how far you fell

a ravaged shell you set about
scheming a new image
a dire attempt to plump and restore
goods shrivelled and yellowed with age

with reptilian ease
you claw your way back
fired up for another go
sans soul which you ceded long ago
for no price was too high to pay
to reassure insecure ego
and revive dead wood
well worn beyond decay.

Heart Problems

It wasn't that she was impossible to love
or difficult
or complicated as he said

the problem was his heart
too small to hold her as she danced with the wind
too cold to catch the fire she lit
too deathly scared to lose sight of the shore
too quick to accept defeat
it wasn't her fault
it wasn't even his
it was simply that he suffered from heart disease

and every attempt he made
pushed his organ to the limit
causing an irreparable glitch
which forced the system to quit.

Never Forever

I will love you forever

soft whispers of night
turn to never

at first hint of morning light.

Fickle

"I love you"
soft as petals

"I do"
prickly thorns.

Shallow End

Hasten not to the light
if you dare not behold what it reveals
for some though blessed with gift of sight
stumble though upright be
tripped by unbridled zeal

heedless of their desperate plight
they sit at table to feast
a man condemned savours his last meal
blind to the signs he missed.

20/20

Dare I say
this was my greatest failure
though not mine alone
for another bears equal or greater share

when two assigned to carry a load
let it fall and crash along the road
which of these could we say did wrong
when both we can see are strong

heavy of heart I declare
if I had to do it again
I'd do so with infinite care
or altogether refrain
for to dare and dare in vain
I couldn't bear the pain.

Cake & Crumbs

We love as if there's a limit
a measure assigned to each
that we fear to deplete

yet love is an infinite feast
a heaving table where all get to sit
with enough for a thousand lifetimes
for the greatest to the least.

Heads & Tails

Love is a four letter word
so is hate
be cautious with the latter
for the former it swiftly desecrates

placed on a scale
one uplifts
the other depletes
it's up to you
which you choose

with love you win
with hate you lose.

Will They

But will they sit with you in the shade
and shield you in the storm

will they hold your hand
when you stumble in the dark
or steady you on shifting sands?

Pieces

Brokenness is that rare gift
that lets the poison flow out
the light flood in
the healing begin.

II

INTO THE DARK

Unspoken

Sometimes
when she opened her mouth to speak
all that came out were tears

that was the only way
she knew to say
she'd lost something very dear.

Remembrance

Love dies
flowers fade
the sun sets
and we, we age

in the end
memories are all that's left
memories are all we have

treasures we carry to the grave
summed up in a tidy epitaph.

In the Ring

Some people may be in your corner
but they don't want you in the fight

they cheer loudest in your hearing
but when you fall
take great delight in your plight

the wise ones were right
know your enemies
but first know your friends
not just by name
get to know their game

it's some of your nearest and dearest
who'll push you off the edge
then watch as you tumble
from dizzying heights.

All the Lonely People

What if all the stars we behold
glowing in the sky
are all the lonely souls below
tears glistening in their eyes?

Into the Dark

Once her vision adjusted, the darkness was not the frightful place she thought it would be. As things took shape she began to see herself in a different light, learning to speak secrets that were never hers to keep. Others, long hidden in their quest for release, found a way to her through the thickest night. Motives buried deep in so many hearts rose unbidden, as memories came flooding back, echoes unchained in time. The further she ventured into the dark, the clearer things became. Where at first she'd rushed, now she lingered. In places where the darkness felt impenetrable, priceless insights emerged like the first glimmers of dawn. It was a giant puzzle coming together. One she never knew existed. Pieces of her self she had never missed were falling into place, coming together to complete the picture. As she made her way, the dots connected with every step, constellations in the sky, mapping her way back to the light.

Comings & Goings

Loneliness was her best friend
Death a constant companion
there was Despair
urging her to take her leave

Joy occasionally surprised her
Peace wrote when she could
promising someday she'd come to stay
Love stood watching at a distance
as Time went rushing by.

Missed Connections

There are hearts that will struggle to love you
there are hearts that will promise
but prove untrue
there are hearts that starved of love
in loving you would have found
their every yearning fulfilled
their joy complete
but you never got to meet
and not knowing what they'd missed
were ever haunted by the feeling
of a life they might have lived.

The Weather Report

Some days all you need
is a good cry
and a hand to hold
to keep you from drowning
in your flood of tears.

Life

Some days the heart sighs
some days the soul sings

some days overflow with sorrow
some days fear crowds into your marrow

some days it feels impossible to hold
all the goodness
the divine unfettered bestows.

Memories of Dreams that Never Were

The ache that naught can cure
the haunting feeling
that will not disappear

flowers that never bloomed
trees that bore no fruit
dreams we trampled underfoot

the certainty
that things could have been different
but never knowing how.

Apologies

Sorry I cannot come
I'm struggling to get out of bed
the ache in my head
resonates like a drum
my body's as heavy as lead
so sorry I cannot come

sorry I can't make the party
I'd so have loved to be there
but the distance from my bed to the shower
when I feel like a car with deflated tires
whose fuel gauge reads empty
so sorry I can't make the party.

Echoes

Sometimes in the thick of night
you'll hear faint echoes go

I love you
I miss you

but only in the darkest dark
for lies cannot withstand the light.

Afraid

Afraid of what they'll say
afraid of what they'll think
knowing they'll do so anyway
whether into emptiness I sink

afraid to speak my thoughts, ideas
that if I do they'll disappear
so afraid I dare not dare
so still I sit and drown in fear

where did it come from
when did you learn to be afraid
was it the silent ghosts or the raging storms
or years of chiding and endless tirades?

The End of Love

Every I love you was a lie
a blindfold leading further into the dark
a lanyard to trip over choke and die
dimming every spark

every I love you was condemnation
to the deepest, darkest place
a sugar coated slap in the face
to distract from their domination

every I love you was a knife through the heart
a crime scene with hard-to-find clues
a bulls eye scored with venomous darts
leaving you black and blue

every I love you frayed the cords
causing the lies to unravel
and despite the pain you could finally afford
a different path to travel.

III

GLIMMERS

Do You

Do you give people too much importance
and yourself none

do you leave your affairs to chance
as you rush off to lend a hand

do you count yourself a priority
a high value asset

or do you consider yourself a nonentity
replaceable, easy to forget.

Vibes

Think twice about whom you allow in

she who says impossible
show her the door

she who says it's possible
give her the floor.

The Dream Killers

A highly underrated skill in life
I've found
is knowing with whom to share
and from whom to withhold your dream

there is the willing midwife
as you birth that fragile thing
then there are those
to keep it forever unseen.

Knowing

You may not know what you want
in a given situation

but it matters too
extremely so
that you know
what it is you don't.

Never Empty

When it feels like all is lost
and only hope remains
even the littlest bit is plenty
to share with one
who's running on empty.

Still Waters

It wasn't that she was strong
it was how well she hid her weakness

it wasn't that she was whole
it was how well she hid her wounds.

Scorched Earth

Some lead nowhere, some to despair. Some cost a heavy toll to cross and they're not worth the loss. Burn the bridges. Some are rickety, worn beyond repair. Burn them without a care. Burn them for they are no longer safe, no longer sound. Set your feet on solid ground. Places, faces, names, the you with whom they played their games, how clear they appear against the flames. Let the fire sear the memories in your mind, the heat hardwire your brain. Toss the ashes to the wind, leaving no trace to lead you back. Feel the burn of lessons learnt and walk away, never to return.

Said Life

I will take you through seasons
and there will be joy
and what you build
I will destroy

and you will sink to murky depths
a figure of scorn
there to weep and mourn
for all that's come to naught

when you come up for air
I will shatter you into shards
grind you fine as dust
and throw you to the wind
and when it blows you back
I will sift then mould you
into something new

I will lift you up
to dine with kings
to ride with knights
soar with angels
and stand with legends

the deeps are shallow
the rivers narrow
shake off your sorrow
you won't need it tomorrow.

Grounded

From birth to death, the one constant in your life is you. Everyone else is only passing through. Some will build you up, some will tear you down, some will only stay a while, some seemingly forever. Some you will love, some you will loathe. Some will leave sorrow and scars, others, sweetness and smiles. All the while there is you; learning, growing. From birth to death, the one constant in your life is the ever changing you. It begins and ends with you.

Giving

When God created us
He gave us two hands
one to juggle our daily plans
the other to aid one
who's caught in quicksand.

Beauty

The beauty of life is
even in the ugly
in the hurt
in the pain
so much beauty
yet remains.

Lenses

It matters not the size of window
if you cannot see the light.

Here's Hoping

I hope when you cry
there will be someone to lean on

I hope when you're hurting
there will be someone to hold you

I hope when you call
someone will hear you

I hope when you're broken
there will be healing
and someone to lead you back to wholeness

and should you find yourself alone
a long way from home
I hope that someone will be you.

Amazing Grace

You couldn't tell from looking
that she'd been through the fire
that more than once she'd died
and in dying been reborn

you couldn't tell from looking
that she'd survived the floods
washed clean, renewed
glowing like the morn

you couldn't tell from looking
the longings of her heart
the failures she'd endured
the losses she had borne

with wisdom she wrestled doubts
with grace she navigated the deep
with patience she nurtured hope
with faith she greeted each new dawn
knowing that every day was a promise fulfilled
a dream to watch unfold.

Carry On

Boundless grace flows
in the depths of despair
as hope runs thin
and doubts mount within

as far as you've fallen
another has fallen further still
who's counting on you to help them up
from the bottom of the deep

you will never be so crushed
that you cannot lift another up
so broken that you cannot build another up
so empty that you cannot fill another's cup
so far gone that you cannot lead another back

find little ways to thrive
in your struggle to survive
even faded flowers flourish
drawing bees from their hives

though it feels like a desolate wasteland
let it spring forth,
a new way of being
for life still blooms in your heart
calling you softly to carry on living.

Travellers

Every soul you meet
as you go your way
travelling different roads
focusing on different goals
all searching for a place to belong
a place to call home.

In Transit

The business of life is to go on
your business is to keep up

you may get off to rest for a while
only to find while you were gone
it moved further along

and so it goes
until one day you get off
never to get on again.

Intuition

There's a time to fly solo
there's a time to run in a pack

better to be delayed in your goals
than to have a knife stuck in your back.

Trusting

The river didn't know how far it had to flow
to make it to the sea

the wind didn't have a destination mapped out
as it blew across the land

the eagle didn't know how high she'd need to fly
to nest at the top of the mountain
nor the salmon
to rise beyond the waterfall

yet off they went
none knowing
each trusting
they'd get to the place they needed to be.

Diamonds All in a Row

They told her to look for the silver lining
but who wants a silver lining
when you can have polished gold
with rubies and diamonds aglow
set row upon row upon row.

Blue Skies Forever

Little girl with your head in the clouds
tripping over roots and rubble and rocks
never once slowing down
never fearing you'll topple your crown

little girl as your story unfolds
from afar we applaud
ever so proud to see
our little girl how she's grown.

Dreamer

I want to go back
and hug that little girl
I want her to know
how much she is loved

I want to tell her she's safe
I want to tell her she counts
I want to tell her she is beautiful
that she belongs

I want to sit with her in a field of wild flowers
clouds shifting as they traverse the blue
as she shares her childish dreams
hoping with all my heart
they'll someday come true

I want to go back
and hold that little girl
write a note and stick it in her heart
so wherever she goes she'll always know
from this one truth she'll never depart
the fact that she is loved.

Dance

There are people who'll kick you off the floor when you'll dance to their tune no more. They'll drag you through the mud, declare you a loon and have nothing to do with you. No matter darling, when they do, make your own music and dance. Dance in the swirl of falling snow. Dance through teeming monsoon. Dance in the corner of a tiny room or wide open fields of bloom. Dance when it shines, dance in the gloom, dance with heaviness in your heart, dance despite the aching parts. Dance through the pain of brokenness, dance through never ending hopelessness. Dance clumsy, dance awkward, dance even when it feels like you're moving backwards, for as long as you keep dancing my darling, every step moves you forward. Close your eyes and gently sway, you'll see the energy make a way. In puddles of tears, overwhelmed with fear, dance for your path to clear. Some days it will be tough to set one foot before the other but even the smallest effort is effort enough. For one day you'll find yourself striding tall, and what a feeling to know that though you faltered, you did not fall, you danced your way to healing. Even on days overwhelmed with feeling, not once did you stop. You danced your way through it all.

Thawing

Winter came and froze me over
couldn't step back couldn’t move forward
night descended like a fresh coat of tar
on a road that stretched forever

in the spring I started to thaw
as the warmth seeped in started moving around
life flowed to places chilled and raw
so healed over scars were all I found

summer issued a reminder
what a thrill to be alive
the sky bluer, the sun brighter
honey bees and humming birds
wild flowers and waterfalls
all saying thrive

let go the past
said Autumn when she came
aged trees nodding their ascent
set the world aflame
no half measures they said
bring your all to the game
live so when you're gone
they'll remember your name.

Burn

They tried to shrink you to the smallest size
around which they could wrap their minds

they tried to paint you over
to dim your shine

they wrote you a script to salve their egos
so you'd blend in with their vapid kind

but you were not born to be bound
and when they set a light to you
and stood back in satisfaction to watch you burn
they saw you come alive
dancing in the flames
unfazed by their virulent games

only then did it dawn on them
how wrong they'd been all along
for as the flames rose higher and higher
they saw it was there you belonged
they saw that you were the fire.

Stories

In the end
the story was about
fixing what was broken
finding what was lost
redeeming what was taken
letting go the cost
and finally learning to live again.

IV

INTO THE LIGHT

Good Morning

Every sunrise is a reason to try again
to salute with confidence the dawn
forgetting what is past

every day brings new gains
where we fall we soldier on
faithful to the last.

Utamu wa Maisha

When the wind tickles the flowers in the fields
and they laughing
call your name
to come out and play
do so without delay

abandon your desk
shoes off your feet
forget memos
and deadlines
and targets to meet

the sun impatient greets you with a kiss
the birds chirp and chitter
as if in laughter
knowing you'll sing off key
the cheeky dust takes delight in your sneeze
as towering trees tease with prickly leaves

cotton clouds enfold you in peace
your heart sighs in bliss
wishing everyday could be like this.

One Day We'll Laugh About It

One day I'll tell you about it Joe
in a place where the earth is red, the grass green
and wild flowers through hedges grow

we will laugh in the stifling heat
over mugs of spicey tea
as we relive the story

we will laugh like hyenas in the wild savannah
feasting on the lions' kill
giddy with glee as we play the reel
retracing a journey mapped in steel

we'll laugh you see
because despite the lows and blows
as the sun sets over the hill
we will savour the thrill of victory.

Twists & Turns

We sing
we laugh
we dance
sometimes we weep

we dream
we dare
we fly
we fall
and sometimes when we can
we live.

Be That Girl

When she laughed
she laughed out loud
so loud you could see to the end of her throat
so loud she once startled a bleating goat

her eyes would shrink to a sliver
she might even shed a tear
her bosom aquiver with infectious cheer
and when she'd come back to herself she'd say
pointing
you'll feel a good laugh in your head
your feet and your liver

she said it was sinful to laugh in whispers
she said, laugh so loud when you're gone
they'll hear echoes and remember
how we climbed mango trees and ate our fill
steeped in sticky juice
how we'd splash in puddles as it poured with rain
trooping home with mud caked shoes
and how some thought she'd gone insane
the night we tainted Aunt Margaret's tea with booze

laugh, she'd say even when you're in pain
it's a way to trick your brain
before you know it you'll be whole again
and laugh she did to her dying day
holding her belly when it ached
as laughing too we watched it shake
as really there wasn't any other way.

Superstar

You are every galaxy
that lights the way
on the path to eternity.

Fresh Faced

Go out and have all the fun
turn out the lights and dance all night
from your moment of birth
till you breathe your last
young is all you'll ever be

though your bones creak
and your vision blur
still you'll be swift and supple
fresh faced as a daisy
through the eye
that only your mind can see.

Come Come

Come sit here a while
I'll tell you all kinds of ways
you're wonderful.

Wondrous

You are weird
you are wild
you are wondrous
you are wonderful

in so many ways
in every way
you are exactly what the world needs
in this moment
on this day.

Inner Space

You are a thousand sunsets
thunder and lightning

you are the nurturing earth
flowing rivers
the breath of God

you are cascading waterfalls
towering trees
ocean depths
heavenly heights
flowers in bloom
mist and dew
you are the universe
and the universe is you.

Precious

All is beauty
and you
you are the most beautiful of all.

Wrapped Up

The greatest gift you'll ever give
is to give to another
of yourself.

Timeless

No heart is ever old
that loves.

Sing Along

Kindness is a language
every heart can speak
a song
every heart can sing.

Sing Your Song

There's a song that only your soul can sing
a melody embossed on your veins
only your heart can play the beat
as lyrics flow unseen
and harmonies rise in soaring waves
from memories within

sing your song
though your voice may break
sing though you miss some notes
sing though it leaves you out of breath
sing your song
like only you can sing.

Flavours

For some people you'll be too sweet
for others too tart
but there are those you've yet to meet
for whom you'll be the perfect blend
to pour without limit
into the pathways of their hearts.

Revelations

Beauty knows my name
she calls and says
let's go discover beautiful places
meet beautiful people
live beautiful lives

she holds the key to ancient mysteries
secrets from antiquity
she says, let us tiptoe through time and see
a different side of me.

Unexpected

Little gems scattered
on the pathway to heaven
often times we fail to see
distracted by illusions
of grandiosity

it may not be the great love you hoped for
but when someone offers their heart
shares their hopes and dreams
secrets and fears

be gentle with them
they've shared a priceless gem.

Cartography

I drew a map of the world
when I stepped back to look
as the image unfurled
it was a picture of you.

Destination

Love is where it begins
love is where it ends
love is everything in between

love is the destination
the eternal question
the axis on which the world spins

everything makes sense
nothing makes sense

in all the muddle
in all the mess
may all the love you ever gave
find its way back to you

in multiple ways
wave upon wave
lapping on the shores of eternity
and bear you gently someday to your grave.

Let Love Lead

Two, step, three, step, four step, turn
you will cha-cha through the fire
waltz unscathed
with neither scratch nor burn

you will rumba through raging waters
dance the cancan on the shore
twist and turn with the tornado
tango westward as it blows

regardless of time and tempo
keep your hand in love's firm hold
follow the current as it flows
love knows where you need to go.

Love Is

Love is two hearts dancing
to a melody only they can hear.

Cadences

I haven't met you
yet I miss you
and every time my heart skips a beat
yours plays an extra one
to fill it in.

Carpe Diem

Let me have a taste of you
for none fills me like you do

let us lie here and dream
in dreaming seize the day

though we are young and limber
let's not for too long linger

for the years fly swift as arrows
and the sun fades into shadows.

X

There they stand
two souls melting
one into the other
softly, sweetly
a kind request
a gentle command
at once an invitation and an offer
to give is to receive
in equal or greater measure
the pleasure derived from these two words
perfectly strung together
"kiss me."

Landing Ground

Love needs a soft place to land
well watered, free of weeds
where it can sow seeds
and sink roots deep

love needs a soft place to land
it's travelled far to find a home
will it find a heart of stone
woebegone that loves to moan
or will it find a place to put forth shoots
and bear an abundance of fruit.

Kiss Kiss

His kisses taste of sunsets and strawberries, warm banana bread, damp forest walks, snow drenched winter mornings, hot chocolate in an oversized mug. They call forth flavours of silvery dew and moonlit hues, baby's breath, corals in the deep, warm waves lapping at her feet on an endless expanse of beach. Every kiss is a dream, a fantasy, it is life and laughter, the promise and the fulfilment, butterflies fleeting from flower to flower, marshmallows melting over a flaming bonfire, conversations that flow for hours, each one a gentle beginning, a glorious ending, with little glimpses of the in between. He tastes of what lies within, places he's been, sights he's seen. He is all she craves with every ounce of her being, everything that makes her heart sing and gives her a sense of belonging, a safe harbour and a launching pad. It is flying, diving, discovering, daring! Each kiss is the sun, the moon, fire and ice, snowflakes and sandstorms, hailstones and hell fire! The meeting of their lips is an expedition launched - a discovery of new worlds, a retelling of the old, of myths and legends steeped in gold. It sates her thirst and fans the flames, a magnetic pull that draws her closer, bids her go further and venture deeper into joy, adventure, buried treasure. Every good thing poured without measure waits in just one kiss.

Slow Motion

These hits and runs
and one night stands
they don't do it for me

let's hold hands
and slow dance
share dreams and long term plans

I know love shouldn't sound
like signing up for a mortgage
where's the romance in that
but you get to that stage
where you need more than a dalliance
a solid foundation not shifting sands

I don't want to fall in love
falling hurts
it's bruises and bleeding and broken bones

oh no
let's not fall in love
let's wrap our souls about each other
and weave dreams to fulfill together.

Navigation

There are many paths to follow
to get you where you want to go
some days you might feel lost
the tracks in the sand too faint to discern

there will be wrong turns and u-turns
doubt infusing detours
dead ends and unexpected bends
towering mountains to tunnel through
and hostile elements sucking the life out of you

there are many paths to follow
to get you where you want to go
but to get where you need to be
follow where love leads

slowly, gently, surely
you will find yourself in that one place
where all along
you belonged.

Spaces

There are places you will thrive
there are places you'll feel buried alive
filled with people beautiful on the outside
as wholesome as cyanide

there are places where they'll smile
at the sound of your name
making room for your narrow frame
where things will feel effortless
there'll be no need to impress

a homecoming long overdue
in countless ways they'll say
this place was incomplete without you
we hope you're here to stay.

Stories

Live not the story the world told of you
it's only half a tale

peppered with half truths and untruths
for which there isn't proof

for how could it know to tell of seeds
sowed in the deep of your soul

all it could write was what it saw
the dirt that hid the gold

so write it anew
the story of you
from an insider's point of view
traversing depths none ever knew
in wholeness make it true.

Certainty

She knew
not knowing how
that everything was going to be alright.

The Return

The journey back is long but not as wearying, for it's a lighter load you bear. Now that you are better prepared; you see the pitfalls from afar. What were stumbling blocks are now stepping stones. The only stops, the places you buried your broken dreams. Crossing the vast emptiness, you pause to collect those which you dared not dream not because they were not destined for you but because you had shrunk to the point that the very idea of fulfilment was ridiculous, frivolous, incredulous even. The journey back bears you to the person you always were but didn't know how to be. There's purpose in every step – the smallest causes seismic shifts, erasing paths you earlier trode, tracing new maps in the mind, infusing joy into places that lay submerged in pain, breathing life into parts dried up and crusted over, allowing yourself the grace to hope, harvesting fruit from the fields of memory, burning down that which no longer serves, sifting the stories you were told to find the kernel of gold that holds the truth. The journey back summons you to the future. A place known yet not, seen yet unseen, treasure buried in the depths of a place called memory. A journey to a place you have never been, yet there lies your origin. How high will you fly? Further than you fell. How deep will you dive? As far as need be, to refill the empty shell. Floating, lighter than air. Free, no sense of despair. There won't be a soul to welcome you home but in the depths of your soul you will know you made it. You will know you're finally there.

What Happened at the End of the Road

At the end of the road
when she'd shed every load
she discovered a new world to explore

at the end of the road she found
that to fall is not to run aground
but an invitation to shift
to reset your compass
rather than aimlessly drift

she discovered that life is a gift to unwrap
to seek beauty
spurn the crap
tread light upon the earth

at the end of the road she embraced her dreams
falling in love with the girl
she'd never got to know

and when there were no more tears to cry
when she'd faced her fears and confronted the lies
she discovered finally that she could fly.

Keep Walking

Keep moving. It doesn't matter how slow you go. What matters is that you're going in the right direction; taking the right path. Don't rush. You'll get lost in the noise and confusion. The world is full of distractions. Listen to your heart. Let your soul chart its course. The journey is yours alone. Don't follow the crowd however tempting, or jump on the first bandwagon, that would be too easy. The destination is yours alone. There will be times you'll want to give up. The challenges will overwhelm you. There are times you will fall and life will callously take your all. There are times you will be hopelessly lost. Let wisdom find you. Let faith lead you. It may take months, years, decades. Don't give up. What is a year in the grand scheme of things? Keep moving. Time moves one second at a time. Progress comes one step at a time. Trust that you will get there not a moment late. You will not be a day early nor a day delayed. It will be as destiny dictates. You won't be too young or too old. You, beautiful soul, will be right on time.

Vignette

Once there was a girl
who travelled the world
searching
but never finding
that one true love

then one day
in a forgettable place
in an unforgettable way
she fell in love with the girl in the mirror
and had an affair to remember

the end.

www.ingramcontent.com/pod-product-compliance
Lightning Source LLC
La Vergne TN
LVHW040942150826
845672LV00002B/504

* 9 7 8 9 9 1 4 4 9 3 5 6 6 *